Barack Obama

A Biography of an American President

Table of Contents

Introduction 1

Chapter 1: Obama's Childhood 5

Chapter 2: Obama's Education 10

Chapter 3: Obama's Career-to-Date 15

Chapter 4: Notable Achievements 23

Chapter 5: Obama's Primary Political Views 32

Chapter 6: How He Came to be President 40

Chapter 7: What Might be Next for Obama 48

Conclusion 57

Introduction

"No matter who you are, what you look like, where you come from, you can make it. That's an essential promise of America. Where you start should not determine where you end up." -
Barack Obama.

Barack Hussein Obama, who served as the President of the United States during its 44th term, became the first African American to serve in the highest office in the country when he was first inaugurated in 2008. The son of a black father raised in a small village in Kenya and a white American mother raised in Hawaii, Obama brought a unique set of experiences to the office. You'll find that his background is the quintessential American story—brought up in a middle-class family, a remarkably strong family, where the power of education and hard work helped him get ahead in life. He is a stark example of the purpose of the Constitution that was written with the hope that the United States of America's leadership would not be limited to only those who are born into wealthy or higher status families.

Obama's parents divorced during his early years. He never had a lasting relationship with his father except for a month when he was ten years old when his father visited America. As he describes in his popular book, *Dreams from My Father*, Obama spent his entire adolescent years trying to navigate identifying with himself as he went through a journey of self-discovery. He was interested in political science and decided to study it in college along with international relations, and soon after, he took up a job as a community organizer. He enrolled in Harvard Law School to make a more meaningful impact on the lives of minorities and less advantaged communities in America. He focused on creating job opportunities for the less fortunate and improving housing conditions by working alongside many churches.

Obama met the smart and promising young lawyer Michelle Robinson during a summer internship in his Harvard Law School days. They married a few years later and had two daughters, Sasha and Malia. As the Senator from Illinois, the willingness to create a better world for his daughters was a driving factor in the most important decisions he made as a lawmaker. The incident that propelled him into the national spotlight as a possible candidate for the upcoming presidency was the Democratic National Convention in 2004 when he gave an amazing speech for John Kerry, the Democratic Party nominee.

Right after Obama's DNC address, many political pundits pronounced him a future president; however, no one expected it to happen until he became more established as a Senator. Abraham Lincoln had delivered his "House Divided" speech in the Old State Capitol Building, and this was also where Obama made his candidacy known to the public. After a heated Democratic primary battle with Hillary Clinton, he won the party nomination. He picked Delaware Senator Joe Biden as his VP running mate. In November 2008, the Obama/Biden ticket was elected to be the President and Vice President of the United States, defeating John McCain, the Arizona Senator, by winning 365 electoral votes.

From the very beginning of his law and legislative career, followed by his presidency, he had an innate ability to connect with people. Even though people tend to vote for issues and causes, he followed people across various demographics that personally connected with him and remained loyal to him throughout both his terms. President Obama took office when the country was amid one of the worst recessions in decades. He took varied and ample measures to recover from the recession and make sure a similar situation would not happen again. He scored several historic achievements during his time in the office and left on a high note.

He signed three signature bills during his first term, including a large stimulus bill as a response to the Great Recession. He also signed a healthcare legislation that made medical care more affordable to millions of people across the country, helping many uninsured Americans have reliable health coverage for the first time in their lives, and a legislation that reformed the nation's financial institution. He also worked towards reducing the pay gap between men and women, pressing for the act of fair pay. Not too long after he took office, he was awarded the Nobel Peace Prize for his extraordinary efforts to strengthen international diplomacy and cooperation between people.

President Obama ran for a second term in 2012 as the incumbent President against Mitt Romney, the Governor of Massachusetts, the Republican nominee at that time, and won by 332 electoral votes to Romney's 206. When he started his second presidential campaign, he had already overseen Osama bin Laden's death. During his presidency, the Middle East was perhaps the most important foreign policy challenge he faced. Obama was also responsible for managing a hostile Iran and played a role in stopping the process of creating nuclear weapons. His administration took on an agreement for climate change, along with a majority of nations across the world, to slow down rapid global warming and lower the emission of greenhouse gases.

Even though President Obama had many achievements under his belt when he left the presidency at the age of fifty-five, he was leaving behind a rather chaotic White House due to the unexpected win of Donald Trump. Immediately after his departure, he announced that his family planned to remain in Washington DC until his younger daughter finished high school. President and Mrs. Obama stayed rather restrained in the first year after they left the White House but started playing a more active role later on. Both of them have since published memoirs and engaged actively in the presidential campaign of Joe Biden and Kamala Harris.

During his eight years in the White House, President Obama brought undeniable stability to the economy, job market, housing market, auto industry, and banks. Moreover, he will always be remembered for his dignity, grace, intelligence, patriotism, and skills as a brilliant orator.

Chapter 1: Obama's Childhood

*"Ua Mau ke Ea o ka 'Āina i ka Pono" The life of the land is perpetuated in righteousness
(The motto of the state of Hawaii)*

Barrack Hussein Obama II was born in Hawaii, The Aloha State, on August 4, 1961. He was named after his father, a Kenyan economist. His father was studying in Hawaii in university when he met Ann Dunham, an anthropology student studying at the same university. They got married shortly after, and Obama was born six months later.

Obama's parents had a rocky relationship from the beginning. Obama Sr. had already been married and left his pregnant wife in Kenya before he moved to Hawaii for his higher education, a fact he withheld from Dunham. Soon after Obama's birth, his mother relocated to Seattle, and she raised him as a single parent. Meanwhile, Obama Sr. completed his degree and enrolled in Harvard University for a MA in Economics program. Obama's parents parted ways and got a divorce in 1964.

Ann Dunham returned to the University of Hawaii to complete her degree. During her first year back, she met Lolo Soetoro, another anthropology student from Indonesia. Soetoro had completed two semesters of his study at Northwestern University and the University of Wisconsin before he arrived at the University of Hawaii. He was a surveyor from Indonesia, studying in Honolulu on a grant from the East-West Center. A hardworking student with huge ambitions, Soetoro completed his master's degree in Geography in 1964, a study area that complemented his surveying career back home.

With shared interests and a passion for making a lasting contribution to society, Dunham and Soetoro had a healthy and happy relationship. They got married in 1965 and lived in Honolulu with young Barack as a family. Since Soetoro was on a student visa, they could only extend his stay for two more years after completing his degree. He left for Indonesia a year after their marriage, with the hope of Dunham and Obama joining him in Indonesia once she completed her degree. Once Soetoro left, Dunham moved in with her parents with her son and continued her studies. Barack started kindergarten in 1966 at Noelani Elementary school in Honolulu. His mother received her Bachelor of Arts degree in Anthropology in 1967.

Four Years in Indonesia

Starting another formative experience in his life, young Obama and his mother flew to Indonesia to join his stepfather in 1967, when he was six years old. They lived in South Jakarta for two-and-a-half years in a newly built and flourishing neighborhood. After getting his MA in Geography, Soetoro had started working for the Indonesian government as a topographic surveyor. With her knowledge in anthropology and innate curiosity to learn about different cultures and experiences, Ann Dunham started working for Indonesia-America Friendship Institute, a US government subsidy. She was also working as an English teacher for Indonesian children.

Obama attended St. Francis of Assisi Catholic School from 1st grade to 3rd grade. The school was nearby their house, and the primary language used in the school was Indonesian. As a quick-learning child, Obama was able to speak in the local language fluently at the time. His old school records show his name as "Barry Soetoro." After two years, he moved to an elementary school where his education mainly consisted of homeschooling, thanks to his mother. Barack speaks about his early school years, recalling how he and his mother woke up early in the morning to study Calvert School, Maryland homeschooling curriculum, before he went to school every day. His mother also used speeches by Martin Luther King Jr. and recordings of Mahalia Jackson to further enrich his homeschooling experience. Obama also speaks fondly about his stepfather, on how he had a "pretty hard-headed assessment of how the world works." In August 1970, Obama's mother and stepfather had a daughter, Maya Kassandra Soetoro.

Life with Grandparents

Although Obama was getting the best education Indonesia had to offer for a young child his age, his mother wanted him to get an American education, especially to prepare him for college. Therefore, she sent him back to Hawaii to live with his grandparents and start his 5th grade in Punahou School, a private college preparatory school in Honolulu. During his prep school days, Barack went by the nickname "Barry." The private prep school had a steep tuition, but Dunham's mother, Madelyn Dunham, was working as a Vice President in Bank of Hawaii, which helped pay the tuition with assistance from a scholarship provided by the school. Obama called his grandmother Toot after the Hawaiian term "tutu," which meant grandmother. She had started working in the bank as a clerk and worked her way up to becoming one of its first two female vice presidents.

Shortly after Obama was back in Hawaii living with his grandparents, his father, Barack Obama Sr., visited him for a month. Since Obama Sr. passed away in 1982 at the age of 48 as a result of a car accident, this visit was the last time Obama would see his father. In his book, *Dreams from my Father*, Obama speaks about meeting his father as a young boy, and the struggle he went through to reconcile the social perceptions that came with his biracial heritage. "My father looked nothing like the people around me," he wrote, "—that he was black as pitch, my mother white as milk—barely registered in my mind." Years later, Obama's half-sister would visit him in Chicago, and he would learn how his father became a heavy drinker and became somewhat of a social outcast during his final years.

In 1972, when Obama's sister was two years old, his mother moved to Hawaii with her to start her graduate studies in Anthropology. The Asia Foundation, a non-profit organization committed to improving lives across developing countries in Asia, supported her graduate studies with a grant. Until Obama was in 8th grade, he lived with his mother and his sister. Ann Dunham completed her master's degree in 1974 and moved back to Indonesia with her daughter to do fieldwork. Young Obama decided to stay with his grandparents and finish high school in Honolulu. His mother spent most of the next 20 years in Indonesia, working towards a Ph.D. degree in Anthropology, which she earned in 1992. She and Soetoro divorced in 1980.

High School Years

Obama's high school years were somewhat tumultuous, just as they are for any teenager trying to find their place in the world. He speaks about drinking alcohol and occasionally smoking marijuana to try to escape from the many questions regarding his father and the confusion he felt trying to blend in with his mother's heritage but never feeling fully comfortable. Since he was admitted to Punahou School thanks to his grandfather's connections, some believed he did not deserve to be there. His grades were also only a little above average, scoring no more than B grades for most of his subjects. He played for the basketball team of his school during his freshman year. As a teenager, most of his time was spent on the beach, at parties, or on the basketball court.

Chapter 2: Obama's Education

"When we study together, we learn together, we work together, and we prosper together." - Barack Obama

Coming from two highly academically accomplished parents, Obama had always been a good student. His mother had closely guided his early years of education, and as he grew up, Obama developed a natural fondness towards gaining knowledge and the process of learning. Just when he was entering school age, he moved to Indonesia with his mother to join his stepfather. He attended local Indonesian schools from the age of six to ten, supplemented by homeschooling by his mother. He was able to speak the Indonesian language fluently due to his time in local schools. He also had a good relationship with his stepfather, who taught him resiliency and how to face the changing world.

High School

Seeing the promising potential of intelligence that she saw in Barack, his mother sent him to start schooling in Honolulu while living with Madelyn and Stanley Dunham, his educated and fairly well-off grandparents. His grandfather's connections as an army veteran and his grandmother's comfortable salary as a higher executive in a bank allowed them to send him to a private college preparatory school, with some help from a partial scholarship awarded by the school as well. He was getting consistent above-average grades during high school, but he was not a straight-A or exceptional student. He completed his high school years there, graduating in 1979.

Occidental College

After his high school graduation, he got a full scholarship to Occidental College, a liberal arts college in LA, California. In his memoir *Dreams from My Father*, he mentions that he selected Occidental over several other respectable colleges he was accepted to because of a girl he met in Honolulu. The girl was vacationing in Hawaii when he met her, and she was living in Brentwood, a neighborhood in LA close to Occidental College.

Young Obama gave his first public speech when he was a student at Occidental College in 1981. He was the opening speaker at a rally held outside the Arthur G. Coons Administrative Center in the college, protesting the investments of Occidental in companies that were doing business in apartheid South Africa, an extreme system of segregation on the grounds of race in the country at the time. Margot Mifflin, an author who was completing her BA degree in English, reminisced about her experience of witnessing Obama's speech in an article published in The New Yorker magazine. She mentioned how he stood with one hand in his pocket, speaking in declarative spurts, but without any signs of the seasoned orator that he would become years later. Before he finished his speech, he was carried off by some students pretending to be oppressive Afrikaners he was rallying against funding. Obama was also into poetry and creative writing during his year at Occidental. Some of his poems were published in the spring 1982 issue of Feast, the school's literary magazine.

An excerpt from his poem "Pop," which was about a special moment between him and his maternal grandfather, Stanley Dunham:

"Sitting in his seat, a seat broad and broken

In, sprinkled with ashes,

Pop switches channels takes another

Shot of Seagrams, neat, and asks

What to do with me, a green young man

Who fails to consider the

Flim and flam of the world, since

Things have been easy for me..."

Obama traveled to Indonesia to visit his mother and Maya, his half-sister, in the summer of his freshman year at Occidental College. He also visited India and Pakistan for several weeks, visiting the families of a few friends he met in college. He also played basketball during his Occidental years and spent "a lot of time having fun," according to him.

Columbia University

In 1981, he transferred to Columbia University, an Ivy League university in New York City as a junior student. The reason for this transfer was the desire to be in a vibrant and urban environment. He majored in Political Science with specialties in International Relations and English Literature. He was living on West 109th street, just off-campus. According to an interview with Columbia College Today newspaper that was published in 2005 after his popular keynote speech at the DNC, Obama said time at Columbia University was rather quiet and focused on studying. "When I transferred, I decided to buckle down and get serious. I spent a lot of time in the library", he says, "I didn't socialize much. I was like a monk." As a college student, Obama was also somewhat involved with the Black Students Organization, especially when it came to anti-apartheid activities. He also found his political voice and wrote to student publications in the university on war and politics. One such article was called "Breaking the War Mentality," published in Sundial, a campus news magazine.

During his years at Columbia University (1982), he learned of the passing of his father, Barack Sr, from a car accident. In 1983, he graduated with a Bachelor of Arts degree with a GPA of 3.7. His job right after college was as a financial researcher and a writer for Business International Corporation. He then worked for New York Public Interest Research Group that was at the City College of New York as a project coordinator for a few months. With a college degree and the ambition to contribute to society, he moved to Chicago in 1985, hoping to work as a community organizer. For three years, he worked as the director of the Developing Communities Project, a faith-based organization.

Harvard Law School

In the fall of 1988, Barack Obama enrolled at Harvard Law School with the hope of being able to facilitate better community organization. His experience as a community organizer in Chicago largely contributed to his decision. Due to his natural charisma as a leader, writing skills, good grades, and studious nature, he was selected as the first black President of the Harvard Law Review at the end of his first year. He oversaw a staff of 80 editors as the editor-in-chief. His history-making position was widely and nationally reported, which led him to get his first book deal. Harvard was the first place where he first became a political sensation and a charismatic leader.

An article published in Harvard Law Bulletin in the fall of 2012 shed some light on Obama's life in Harvard Law School as a student. It mentioned how he was universally well-liked and respected and showed a certain maturity and wisdom beyond his years. During Obama's time at Harvard Law School, there had been certain turbulence with rallies and protests due to the faculty's lack of diversity. While Obama supported the student protests at the time, he had a nuanced and insightful view of such protests, according to Anthony Brown, the congressman for Maryland's 4th district, who was a fellow student in Harvard Law School with Obama. Another fellow student, Kenneth W. Mack, a historian and current Professor of Law at Harvard, recalls how, "when Barack spoke, people listened," a recurring expression by many when Obama was a presidential candidate, and eventually when he became POTUS.

Chapter 3: Obama's Career-to-Date

"A change is brought about because ordinary people do extraordinary things." - Barack Obama

From idyllic sunny beaches in Hawaii to 1600 Pennsylvania Avenue, Barack Hussein Obama has had an illustrious professional career. He has been a community organizer, Law and Government lecturer, Civil Rights Attorney, and legislator in the Illinois Senate and the US Senate before he took up the job of Commander-in-Chief of the United States of America. He reminisces how every job he did during his college years up until he started his first presidential run has been valuable in preparing him for the position of the leader of the Free World. That included everything from implementing and enforcing laws, directing the federal government's executive branch, and commanding the armed forces to conduct the US foreign policy.

Community Organizer

After graduating from Columbia University, he spent a few years working as a researcher and writer while trying to discover the career path he ultimately wanted to take. Community organizing was a career option he kept coming back to, which led him to apply for several projects in locations with people who could benefit from community organizing projects. Shortly after, a church-based community organization called Developing Communities Project hired him as the director. The project covered a total of 8 Catholic parishes, including West Pullman, Roseland, and the South Side of

Chicago, coincidentally the place where his future wife had grown up.

For three years, from 1985 to 1988, Obama worked tirelessly to improve the Developing Communities Project's scope and impact. During his tenure, he started a college preparatory tutoring program for high school-aged children, inspired by the way he benefited during his high school years from such a program. Other initiatives he set up included a job training program and a tenant's rights organization. His affinity towards these social causes would be further exemplified later on when he ran for office. At the same time, he was also working as an instructor and consultant for a community-based organization known as the Gamaliel Foundation, which provided consulting services and training for congregation-based community organizations.

He traveled abroad to Europe and then to Kenya in 1988, where he saw his paternal relatives for the first time. He spent three weeks in Europe and a little over a month in Kenya. After he came back, he enrolled at Harvard Law School. Due to his impressive student record at Columbia University, he had also received a full scholarship to the Northwestern University School of Law as well. In one of his first political endeavors, he was selected to be the Harvard Law Review editor in his first year, serving as the President of volume 104.

Summer Associateship

During his summers as a law student, Obama worked at the Chicago law firms Sidley Austin, and Hopkins and Sutter. During his time at Sidley Austin LLP, he met Michelle Lavaughn Robinson, then 25, an associate at the firm and his future wife. Michelle, who was also a Harvard Law School graduate and working on marketing and intellectual property law, was assigned to be the mentor for Obama. They got engaged in 1991 and were married a year later.

Law and Government Lecturer - University of Chicago Law School

After graduating, he had a Juris Doctor degree with magna cum laude from Harvard Law School in 1990; Obama's first job was as a Visiting Law and Government Fellow at the University of Chicago Law School. He was also working on his first book, *Dreams from My Father,* at the same time. He was teaching constitutional law in UCLS, a job he continued until 2004 when he was elected as a United States Senator. He was promoted to a lecturer position from Visiting Fellow in 1992 and then to a Senior Lecturer from 1996 until he left.

Project Vote

While he was working as a lecturer in UCLS, Obama joined Project Vote, a non-profit voter registration campaign with the aim of having up to 15 thousand of over 400 thousand unregistered African Americans in the state of Illinois become registered. The organization carried out a highly successful Chicago voter registration drive, which led Obama to being named in the "40 under Forty" list in Crain's Chicago Business weekly business newspaper.

Civil Rights Attorney

Obama joined Davis, Miner, Barnhill, and Galland, in 1993, a Chicago law firm specializing in civil rights litigation, as an associate. He spent three years there as an associate and as of counsel from 1996 to 2004. One of the cases he worked while working as a civil rights attorney was a class action suit that was filed against Citibank Federal Savings Bank. The lawsuit alleged that the bank had knowingly engaged in several practices forbidden under the Fair House Act of 1968 and the Equal Credit Opportunity Act of 1974. The case's final judgment was issued with the bank agreeing to pay attorney fees, and the case was settled out of court.

Obama was also a member of the board of directors of the Woods Fund of Chicago, a private independent foundation that worked towards increasing opportunities for less advantaged communities in Chicago. He was a part of other projects and foundations that included the Chicago Annenberg Challenge, a Chicago public school reform project. All this social and civil litigation work paved the path to this political career that began in 1996.

State Senator of Illinois

The first step in Barack Obama's political career was the Illinois Senate. He was elected in 1996, succeeding Alice Palmer, who was disqualified from running in the Democratic primary due to inconsistencies in her petition signatures. Obama represented the 13th District of Illinois, which included Chicago South Side neighborhoods such as Hyde Park, Kenwood, South Shore, and Chicago Lawn. He focused mostly on reforming ethics and health care during his tenure, gaining bipartisan support for legislation that he sponsored.

Some of the laws that he sponsored included increasing tax credits for low-income workers, promoting increasing subsidies for childcare, and negotiating welfare reform. He was the co-chairman of the Joint Committee on Administrative Rules in 2001, a bipartisan committee in which he supported the payday loan regulations as well as regulations for predatory mortgage lending practices put forth by Republic Governor George H. Ryan. After two years of successful work in the state senate, he was re-elected in 1998 and again in 2002. He also had a failed congressional run for Illinois's 1st congressional district in 2000. He lost to Bobby Rush, a four-term incumbent.

Democrats gained the majority in the Illinois state senate in 2002, and Obama was made the chairman of the Health and Human Services committee. One of the major bipartisan legislation he led as the chairman was monitoring racial profiling. The passage of legislation required the police to record the race of the drivers that they detained. Another legislation he sponsored made Illinois the first state to mandate the videotaping of homicide interrogations. During his three terms, Obama made significant progress in the areas of health care, labor, welfare, community investment, law enforcement, campaign finance reform, and more. After he was elected to the United States Senate in 2004, Obama resigned from the Illinois Senate.

Obama started considering a US Senate run in 2002. He enlisted David Axelrod, a political strategist and consultant, to prepare for the campaign. Obama spoke with Jesse Jackson Jr., the Democratic congressman representing Illinois's 2nd congressional district, and informed him that he was not going to run if Jackson was considering a run. Once Jackson informed him that he had already decided not to run, in 2003, Barack officially declared that he was running. From the onset of the campaign, Axelrod ran a strategic advertising campaign that boosted Obama's candidacy. The ads contained an early endorsement by Sheila Simon, the daughter of the late Paul Simon, former US Senator for Illinois, and images of the late Chicago Mayor, Harold Washington.

In the Democratic Senate Primary held in March 2004, Obama received over 52% of the vote. Obama was prepared to have a Republican opponent in the general election. Jack Ryan, the primary winner of the Republican Party, withdrew from the race a few months before the general election, and he was replaced by Alan Keyes, a conservative political activist. Keyes was a long-time resident of Maryland, but he established legal residency in Illinois with his nomination. Prior to the general election, Keyes and Obama had three public debates, expressing stark opposing views on a number of topics, including gun control, tax cuts, stem cell research, abortion, and more.

Obama won the general election with 70% of the votes, which is the largest victory margin for a statewide race in the history of Illinois.

US Senator from Illinois

Barack Obama began his United Senate career in January 2005, as the fifth-ever African-American Senator in US history, and just the third to have been elected popularly. Even though he was a newcomer to Washington, he had recruited a team of qualified advisers and staffers early on. His team members included Pete Rouse, a 30-year national politics veteran as the

Chief of Staff, and Karen Kornbluh, a veteran economist as his policy director. He also hired several Clinton admin officials, including Anthony Lake, Susan Rice, and Samatha Power, for high-level positions.

His senate committee assignments included Health, Foreign Relations, Veterans' Affairs, Education, Labor and Pensions, Homeland Security, and Governmental Affairs. Obama was the chairman of the subcommittee on European Affairs. He was also a member of the Congressional Black Caucus, a caucus made up of African-American members of the United States Congress. Obama was loyal to his democratic and liberal roots when it came to voting during his tenure. From January 2005 until November 2008, he supported 147 bills and 689 sponsorships, including the Federal Funding Accountability and Transparency Act of 2006.

Right after he was assigned to work in the 109th Congress, Obama took an active role in border security and immigration reform. He reached across the aisle and co-sponsored the Secure America and Orderly Immigration Act, an immigration reform bill introduced by Republican Senator from Arizona John McCain, who would later become his opponent in the 2008 presidential campaign. Obama's foreign trips as a member of the Senate's Foreign Relations Committee included trips to Africa, Europe, and the Middle East. Democrats took control of the 110th Congress in 2007, and Obama worked to eliminate travel gifts on corporate jets for Congress members by lobbyists. He also co-sponsored S.453 (Deceptive Practices and Voter Intimidation Prevention Act of 2007) with Sen. Chuck Schumer from New York. The bill proposed criminalizing deceptive practices in federal elections, including automated phone calls and fraudulent flyers.

After he was elected to POTUS in November 2008, Obama resigned his Senate seat, which former Illinois Attorney General Roland Burris replaced.

Chapter 4: Notable Achievements

"Keep exploring. Keep dreaming. Keep asking why. Don't settle for what you already know. Never stop believing in the power of your ideas, your imagination, your hard work to change the world." - Barack Obama.

During his 8 years of presidency, President Obama had many notable achievements. As the first African-American President of the United States, he had a unique responsibility to bring lasting change that positively affected minorities and the entire country. He took office during a time the country was suffering from a terrible recession and changing cultural demographics. His achievements over the years have made him one of the most transformative presidents in modern history. Moreover, his administration was notable for its stable nature, and he was able to achieve several significant accomplishments during his tenure.

First 100 Days

The phrase "first 100 days" was introduced by Franklin Roosevelt, the 32nd POTUS. Many years later, American presidents still use their first 100 days to introduce and enact some of the most ambitious changes at the very start of their term, mostly to show the public how they intend to hit the ground running. President Obama's first 100 days were notably quite productive.

During his first term, he introduced the American Recovery and Reinvestment Act of 2009, a stimulus package as a response to the Great Recession that was inherited from the previous administration. He also signed the Lilly Ledbetter Fair Pay Act, relaxing the statute of limitations for equal-pay lawsuits. Healthcare reform was another important legislation that he introduced during his first 100 days, a cause that he significantly focused on during his entire tenure as POTUS. He supported the UN declaration of sexual orientation and gender identity, making huge strides for the LGBTQ community of the country. While he broke from many Bush administration policy fronts, he followed through on the withdrawal of US troops from Iraq.

Great Recession

The Great Recession was a drastic global economic decline that occurred between 2007 and 2009, starting during the Bush administration. The causes for the recession were a series of events that began with the US housing bubble bursting. Obama's approach to solving this major economic crisis included measures to both ends of the Great Recession and ensuring that it would not happen again. Passing the American Recovery and Reinvestment Act was one of the few major actions he took during the first few months of his administration.

The Recovery Act was a bold fiscal stimulus that included $787 billion in tax cuts and spending. It focused on the people most directly harmed by the recession, especially in the states and local governments suffering the most. He gave relief payments and tax cuts for American families, and the investment projects included clean energy manufacturing along with building roads and bridges for more efficient economic movement. The Obama administration also worked with the Federal Reserve to help repair the country's damaged financial system. There was also a program that helped homeowners facing foreclosures.

Affordable Care Act

Healthcare reform was President Obama's most prominent domestic priority. The Affordable Care Act was the major bill enacted by the 111th Congress and signed into law by him, widely known as "Obamacare." It had a significant regulatory overhaul and expansion of coverage for Americans, reducing a substantial amount of the uninsured population in the country. The law intended to constrain costs of healthcare and improve its quality.

The Affordable Care Act retained most of the existing structures of national health insurance programs such as Medicare, and employer-given health coverage, but the individual insurance markets were overhauled largely. Perhaps the most noteworthy aspect of Obamacare was the mandate for private insurers to accept all applicants without unfair charges for pre-existing conditions and different demographical statuses, except for an applicant's age.

There was strong political opposition for Obamacare, including calls for repeal and legal challenges from private insurers. There were also technical difficulties on the website for the federal health insurance exchange, HealthCare.gov, which were resolved later, but made a less than perfect first impression. However, The Affordable Care Act led to more Americans having affordable health insurance and other benefits such as the lower costs of prescription drugs.

Climate Change

The Obama Administration had a fairly progressive environmental policy. Obama recognized climate change and global warming as one of the most crucial long-term threats facing the world. In 2009, the House passed the American Clean Energy and Security Act in the Senate. However, Senate republicans strongly opposed it since the legislation required the US to drastically cut greenhouse emissions. However, in his second term, Obama announced that he was bypassing Congress and ordering the Environmental Protection Agency to implement the carbon emission limits. Obama unveiled the Clean Power Plan in 2015, a policy that was aimed at combating climate change by reducing greenhouse gas emissions in the US by up to 28% by the year 2025.

He also imposed strict regulations on harmful substances such as sulfur, soot, and mercury that directly affect climate change, and encouraged the country to transition away from coal as an energy source. In 2015, nearly every country in the world agreed to a landmark climate deal at the United Nations Climate Change Conference. Following that, Obama entered the Paris Agreement, which created a universal accounting system for emissions, requiring countries to monitor their own emissions.

The Killing of Osama Bin Laden

On May 2, 2011, Osama Bin Laden, the leader of the al-Qaeda– a militant Sunni Islamist organization–was killed by a successful operation launched by the Obama Administration. Bin Laden was responsible for many horrific terrorist attacks, including the September 11 attacks that resulted in close to 3000 fatalities. The operation code-named as "Operation Neptune Spear" was led by the CIA and Joint Special Operations Command, which included a special team of US Navy SEALs. Another team involved was the 160th Special Operations Aviation Regiment, which was also known as "Night Stalkers."

Bin Laden's compound was in Pakistan, and the raid was launched from Afghanistan. After Bin Laden's body was taken to Afghanistan for identification, the US forces buried it at sea within 24 hours in accordance with Islamic tradition. President Obama addressed the nation at 11:35 pm that day, appearing on all major television networks.

"Tonight, I can report to the American people and to the world that the United States has conducted an operation that killed Osama bin Laden, the leader of al-Qaeda, and a terrorist who was responsible for the murder of thousands of innocent men, women, and children..." (ctd.) - President Obama's Address

LGBTQ Rights

Barack Obama was a pioneering President for expanding LGBTQ rights in the United States. Shortly after he took office, he signed Matthew Shepard and James Byrd Jr. Hate Crimes Prevention Act. The act was a response to the murders of

Matthew Shepard and James Byrd Jr. Shepard due to their homosexuality. The act expanded hate crime laws to cover crimes committed because of a victim's real or perceived sexual orientation.

Another major LGBTQ-related legislation under Obama was the Don't Ask, Don't Tell Repeal Act of 2010. It ended the military's policy of discouraging openly gay members from serving in the United States Armed Forces. He also actively worked towards banning discrimination against employees on the basis of gender or sexual identity. The Obama administration issued many executive orders that helped LGBTQ Americans. He appointed Todd M. Hughs to the Court of Appeals for the Federal Circuit, making him the first openly gay judge in US history.

On June 26, 2015, the United States Supreme Court confiscated all state bans on same-sex marriage, legalizing it in all fifty states. President Obama was the first sitting president to support same-sex marriage.

DACA (Deferred Action for Childhood Arrivals)

In 2012, President Obama introduced Deferred Action for Childhood Arrivals (DACA). This immigration policy allowed individuals brought to the US as children to become eligible for a work permit. The program required the recipients not to have any felonies on their records. The Republican Party largely criticized the policy. This immigration policy followed the DREAM Act introduced to the Senate in 2001, which did not pass. DACA did not include a path to citizenship for recipients as included in the DREAM Act but was created after acknowledging that the "Dreamers"– or the young people brought to the US and raised in the country needed some way to be granted legal status.

President Obama announced the DACA policy with a speech in the Rose Garden of the White House on June 15, 2012, the 30th anniversary of Plyler v. Doe, a Supreme Court decision barring public schools from discriminating against or charging tuition from undocumented immigrant children.

Trade Agreements

The Obama administrations pursued several successful free trade agreements similar to its predecessor. In 2011, the US entered into several free trade agreements with South Korea, Panama, and Colombia. Since the Bush administration originally negotiated these agreements, they were largely supported by the republicans, while the democrats had mixed opinions. Obama reopened the negotiations started by the Bush admin and changed some terms of each deal.

An important multilateral free trade agreement promoted by Obama was the Trans-Pacific Partnership (TPP), which included eleven Pacific Rim countries, including Canada, Japan, and Mexico. During the Bush administration, the negotiations were started, and the Obama administration continued them as a part of their long-term global economic strategy. He sought to refocus the strategy on the growing economies in East Asia, especially Japan. The agreement had goals to establish free-market capitalism as a main normative platform in the region, guaranteeing standards on intellectual property rights and more.

Nomination of Sonia Sotomayor

During his tenure, President Obama made two successful appointments to the US Supreme Court. His first appointment was Judge Sonia Sotomayor, which was historic since she is the first Hispanic and Latina member of the Court. Sotomayor had graduated summa cum laude from Princeton University, and she had received her Juris Doctor from Yale Law. Kirsten Gillibrand and Chuck Schumer, who are both senators in New York, came up with a joint letter to President Obama, asking that he place Sotomayor to the Supreme Court if an opening came up during his term.

After Justice David Souter's retirement, the White House contacted Sotomayor about her possible appointment for the position. On May 26, 2009, President Obama nominated her. She had widespread support from the liberals, with some criticism from conservatives due to several remarks early in her career and her stance on gun ownership. In July 2009, Senate Judiciary Committee voted 13-6 in favor of her confirmation, and the full Senate confirmed her by a vote of 68-31.

Nobel Peace Prize

In 2009, President Obama won the Nobel Peace Prize for his amazing progress towards strengthening cooperation between people and international diplomacy. Obama's promotion of nuclear nonproliferation and his international relations efforts were a large reason for this prize, as announced by The Norwegian Nobel Committee. He acknowledged the news in remarks given at the White House Rose Garden, saying he was surprised and deeply humbled to have been recognized. He added how the Nobel Peace Prize had been awarded not just to honor one specific achievement but to give momentum to a set of causes.

Obama accepted the prize in Oslo in 2009, followed by a speech in which he discussed the tensions between peace and war. His win's reactions were mixed, some calling it a "stunning surprise" while others were criticizing how Obama had not made any major foreign policy achievements since he was less than a year into his first term when he received the prize. Obama became the fourth POTUS to win the Nobel Peace Prize.

Chapter 5: Obama's Primary Political Views

"There is not a liberal America and a conservative America. There is the United States of America. There is not a black America, a white America, a Latino America, an Asian America. There's the United States of America." - Barack Obama.

Barack Obama has held mostly left-leaning centrist views, with many values in alignment with the Democratic platform. The entire Obama administration's general agenda included reviving the economy, providing affordable healthcare to all, and strengthening public education and social security systems. Some of the most progressive agendas included defining a clear path to energy independence and tackling climate change. They also campaigned to end the war in Iraq responsibly and finish the American mission in Afghanistan while working with US allies to prevent Iraq from developing nuclear weapons.

Economic Policy

President Barack Obama came to power when the USA was at the depths of the Great Recession. The country was going through a financial crisis from the year 2007. One of his immediate economic actions was to enact an $800 billion stimulus program called the American Recovery and Reinvestment Act. It was developed as a direct response to the Great Recession, and the primary objective of this act was to save existing jobs and create new ones as soon as possible.

Under his administration, the US economy started creating new jobs consistently from early 2011, which continued throughout his tenure.

His Patient Protection and Affordable Care Act covered over 23 million people with health insurance. The Congressional Budget Office declared that the act moderately reduced the deficit due to the tax hikes on high-income taxpayers. Another important act President Obama signed into law was Dodd-Frank Wall Street Reform and Consumer Protection Act, which overhauled financial regulation and limited bank risk-taking. In 2012, President Obama signed the American Taxpayer Relief Act, which addressed the expiration of Bush's tax cuts. The act allowed those tax cuts to expire for the highest-income taxpayers, and a spending cap was implemented to reduce the deficit.

Another important economic priority that President Obama focused on was income and wealth inequality. He increased taxes on higher-income taxpayers and invested in infrastructure to create middle-class jobs. To address the income inequality before taxes, he also promoted a federally mandated increase in the minimum wage, which did not get support from the Republican Congress. However, eighteen states across the US increased their minimum wages under him, which benefited over 7 million workers. By the end of President Obama's second term, he had record levels of job numbers, median household income, stock market, and household net worth. The unemployment rate was also well below the historical average.

Immigration Policy

President Obama's legacy on immigration is somewhat mixed, with both wins and losses throughout the eight years that he held office. He approached this nuanced issue with the complexity that it deserved. He strictly enforced immigration laws and put forth thoughtful executive actions that shielded many immigrants, especially those brought to the US as children, from being deported. From the very beginning of the Obama administration, there was a focus towards comprehensive immigration reform. Obama's approach towards undocumented immigrants who have successfully contributed to the US economy was less about criminalizing and deporting them and more about providing them a practical path to citizenship. He believed that mass deportation would be not only impossible in logistical terms but also unethical, especially for those who have been brought to the country as children and were now leading model lives.

Despite his continuous effort, Congress did not pass a comprehensive immigration bill during Obama's presidency, which led him towards taking executive actions. In 2010, he supported the DREAM Act but was not able to get it passed in the Senate. Through executive actions, he implemented the DACA policy in 2012, which protected over 700,000 immigrants, mostly young students, whose parents had brought to the United States before their 16th birthday. He tried to protect another four million from being deported through executive actions in 2014, but the Supreme Court blocked it.

The number of deportations under President Obama was high during his first four years, but the numbers fell during his second term. In 2015, it was reported that the percentage of foreign-born people living in the United States was at an all-time high. During the same year, Obama announced that he planned to resettle at least 10,000 Syrian refugees in the United States.

Foreign Policy

When he came into power in 2009, President Obama inherited two wars from the previous administration — the Iraq War and the Afghanistan War, along with many aspects of the ongoing war on terror. Obama's first major foreign policy speech was during his presidential campaign, which focused on bringing a responsible end to the war in Iraq. As President, he oversaw the gradual removal of US soldiers in Iraq. By December 2011, almost all the troops in Iraq were withdrawn. During his second term, he also removed a large number of US soldiers from Afghanistan as well. He presided over the mission that killed al-Qaida leader Osama Bin Laden and reduced the number of prisoners at the Guantanamo Bay detention camp.

President Obama elaborated on his foreign policy during his inaugural address, in which he mentioned lessening the nuclear weapon threat in the world by working with allies. He also extended a friendly invite to the Muslim world, asking to seek a new way forward based on mutual interest and respect. Arab Spring was another important foreign event experienced by the Obama administration. It was a series of anti-government protests that started happening across Africa and the Middle East. President Obama helped organize an intervention in Libya, led by NATO, which resulted in the fall of the long regime by Muammar Gaddafi.

As the first African American POTUS, he prioritized developing a comprehensive Africa policy that included fighting poverty and expanding prosperity in the region. He appointed Susan Rice, a former assistant secretary of state for African affairs, as the US Ambassador to the United Nations, as a way to prioritize the continent. Secretary of State Hillary Clinton worked towards balancing American foreign policy to give much-needed emphasis to booming Asia, investing in diplomatic, economic, and strategic ways to have better US relations in the Asia-Pacific region. Hillary Clinton's first foreign policy tour as the Secretary of State was to Asia, with stops in Japan, Indonesia, China, the Philippines, and South Korea.

Energy Policy

Clean Energy was a novel and important focus in the Obama administration, an issue that was interconnected with many other aspects, from the economy to climate change and job numbers. Many of the Obama administration's energy-related actions were included in the American Recovery and Reinvestment Act of 2009

The White House Office of Energy and Climate Change Policy was a new office President Obama established in the White House. He assigned Carol Browner, a former admin of the Environmental Protection Agency, as the Assistant to the President for Energy and Climate Change. Moreover, soon after the inauguration in 2009, a Special Envoy for Climate Change was appointed by the Secretary of Hillary Clinton. Launching Advanced Research Projects Agency-Energy was a special initiative by Obama with regard to energy. The agency was under the Department of Energy and Department of Defense, promoting and funding research and development of advanced energy technologies.

Nuclear power plants were one of President Obama's prominent suggestions for clean energy. However, in the aftermath of the Japanese Earthquake and Tsunami that happened in 2011, concerns were raised about California's nuclear plants since a similar natural disaster could potentially affect them. Peterson, a US Berkeley professor and former Chair of Nuclear Engineering, reassured that such a situation is unlikely in the US. Creating a self-sustaining home energy efficiency retrofit industry was another energy initiative under President Obama. He also introduced new efficiency standards for home appliances to reduce energy waste and extreme energy consumption. A National Fuel Efficiency Policy was introduced to increase cars' fuel efficiency from 2012 to 2016. Special attention was given to increasing the production of biofuels and creating a renewable fuel standard. President Obama also created a task force to help create a federal strategy for carbon capture and storage.

Social Policy

Social policies include human needs for security, education, work, health, and wellbeing. The Obama administration had progressive and liberal stances on most social issues, including on rather controversial issues such as abortion, sexuality, embryonic stem cell research, and more. President Obama was pro-choice, mentioning in one of his responses to a survey that "Abortions should be legally available in accordance with Roe v. Wade." As a candidate, he was endorsed by several pro-choice groups and organizations, including Planned Parenthood. He has consistently supported a woman's right to choose when it comes to medical care. As a Senator, Obama was a co-sponsor of the Stem Cell Research Enhancement Act, which involved scientifically worthy human stem cell research to the extent permitted by law.

As a presidential candidate, Obama was the first to issue a statement regarding disability community issues. He expressed support for the ADA Restoration Act and the intention to be a part of the Convention on the Rights of Persons with Disabilities. Another progressive social policy he promoted was Sex Education, which was not an issue most administrations addressed. Even when he was a senator in Illinois, he supported a bill that promoted age and developmentally appropriate sex education.

President Obama also worked towards removing the stigma against HIV by taking HIV tests during his visit to Kenya and at the Global Summit on AIDS and the Church. Another social policy that he took as a presidential candidate was stating that he would end the DEA raids on medical marijuana suppliers. He called for Congress to work towards better voting rights and access, especially for minority communities. He supported full representation in Congress for residents of the District of Columbia since residents of Washington DC do not have any voting representation in Congress. Another social aspect he was progressive about was religion, and he encouraged democratic lawmakers to reach out to evangelical Christians and other churchgoers, who are often conservative in their political beliefs, to communicate with them and understand their concerns.

Law Enforcement Policy

In 2006, then-Senator Obama voted in favor of the USA PATRIOT Act, which focused on expanding the law enforcement's abilities to use advanced surveillance to intercept and obstruct terrorism. He voted to reauthorize the act with some amendments that clarified the rights of the individual under surveillance. He was against extending the provision that would give the FBI the authority to conduct what is known as "roving wiretaps." Another important law enforcement policy vote by him was to restore habeas corpus, reporting unlawful detention, to the people detained by the US. He also advocated closing the Guantanamo Bay detention camp.

His stance on the death penalty was that it is used too inconsistently and frequently by the US justice system. However, he did not advocate for fully eliminating the death penalty. His view was that it was a case-by-case issue, in which it can be justified when the community requires to express the full measure of its outrage in certain criminal cases such as "mass murder, the rape, and murder of a child" and similar heinous crimes. As a presidential candidate, he stated in the debates that when it comes to selecting judges as the President, he will look for those with outstanding judicial records and intellect and a sense of what the real-life citizens are going through. He further emphasized that he would look for a person with empathy, heart, and the ability to recognize what it is like to be a young teenage mom or poor, gay, disabled, old or African American.

Chapter 6: How He Came to be President

"Change will not come if we wait for some other person or some other time. We are the ones we have been waiting for. We are the change that we seek." - Barack Obama.

During his 2015 State of the Union Address, President Obama had a great response to the Republicans, who rudely applauded when he said he had no more campaigns to run. He paused for a second, smiled, and quipped, "I know because I won both of them," which gained an even louder applause and good-humored laughter from everyone.

Barack Obama ran two successful presidential campaigns and several other political campaigns before that, which propelled him to become a legitimate candidate for POTUS in a mere four years after he became a US senator. He came into power at the early stages of digital advertising, which he strategically used to create a national presence. Most of his campaign contributions came from small donors from across the country, giving him a chance to not depend too much on large and corporate donors. His 2008 and 2012 presidential campaigns remain to be two of the most successful campaigns to this day. They have inspired many politicians around the world, including Justin Trudeau, the prime minister of Canada, as mentioned in Obama's new memoir "A Promised Land."

2008 Presidential Campaign

When Barack Obama told the public about his candidacy, he was a junior US senator from Illinois. At the Old State Capitol building, he declared his candidacy with his wife and two daughters by his side. This was where Abraham Lincoln gave his famous "House Divided" speech. At the beginning of the campaign, the front-runner was Hillary Clinton, who would later become the Secretary of State under the Obama administration. However, a strategic early primary campaign led by David Plouffe, the campaign manager, and David Axelrod, the media strategist, gave him his first win, which propelled him to become a top-tier candidate.

Further, the support that Obama received from Ted Kennedy and Tom Daschle undoubtedly helped him gain prominence in a crowded field. The momentum gained from the Iowa win led to a number of victories that brought the campaign to Super Tuesday with a legitimate chance of winning. Due to the nationwide campaign that he ran without focusing only on the populous states like most presidential candidates, Obama had massive success in largely rural states, while Clinton's campaign had wins in more populous, urban and coastal areas. Thanks to the digital campaign using early social media platforms such as MySpace, Obama had a lot of small-dollar donations, especially from young people and minorities who connected to his youth and progressive ideas as opposed to a Washington insider such as Clinton.

Although Obama lost the Indiana primary, winning the North Carolina primary gave him the lead. This led to superdelegates endorsing Obama. When he won Oregon, he got the absolute majority, and he started focusing on the general election; and in June, Hillary Clinton showed great support for Obama after ending her candidacy. She would continue to work to get him elected in the general election that followed. In August at the DNC, Barack Obama was officially nominated to be elected as the President of the US. Since John McCain had already passed the delegate threshold and become the apparent Republican nominee a few months back, Obama was somewhat behind in his campaign work for the general election.

The rest of the month, Obama and Hillary ran several events together, encouraging Hillary supporters to back Obama. Starting from July, the Obama campaign had an extremely heavy schedule of fundraising events, attracting big Democratic donors who had backed the Clinton campaign early on. When it was becoming apparent that Obama would win the nomination, there was much excited speculation as to who he would pick as the running mate. There was a lot of urging from the public for him to go for a "unity ticket" with Hillary Clinton. Another possible candidate included Delaware Senator Joe Biden, who was close friends with Republican nominee John McCain. Other possible options were Indiana Senator Evan Bayh, Kansas Governor Kathleen Sebelius, and Virginia Governor Tim Cain, who later became the running mate of Hillary Clinton in her 2016 presidential campaign.

On August 21, 2008, Obama mentioned that he had chosen his running mate and encouraged his supporters to sign up to his campaign's text messaging system to get notified immediately when he makes the formal announcement. There was a large surge of sign-ups for campaigns from both the democrats and republicans since there was also a more entertainment appeal and celebrity that the Obama campaign gained throughout their primary run. The Obama campaign announced Joe Biden has Obama's VP and running mate on his official campaign website, and the supporters were notified by a mass text message. The reason they selected the Delaware senator, according to the campaign, was that blue-collar Americans could relate to him. He also had connections in Capitol Hill as a long-term senator and had personal foreign policy connections and experience, which Obama lacked at the time.

One of the major attacks McCain's campaign had on Obama was his lack of experience in his foreign policy and being a diplomat. Therefore, in the middle of the general campaign, the Obama campaign organized an expansive Middle Eastern and European tour that included countries such as Afghanistan, Kuwait, Iraq, Israel, Germany, France, and Britain. In Berlin, he delivered the speech "A World that Stands as One" before a massive crowd of over two hundred thousand. This tour largely faded out the remarks by his opponents that Obama did not have the capability to portray America as a respected leader on the world stage.

From the time that major party nominees were established until the general election, there were three presidential debates. The debates were done only between Obama and McCain, and no other third-party or independent candidates were invited to the debates. The first debate was in September at the University of Mississippi, in a traditional debate format. The second debate, which was held in October at Belmont University in Nashville, was held in a town hall format. The third debate was a week later in Hofstra University, New York, and held in a seated talk show format with Bob Schieffer of CBC. During the debates, both candidates were quite respectful towards each other, and Obama appeared to be quite informed and confident on the issues and solutions he was putting forth. The turning point of the general election campaign of Obama was when John McCain did not have clear suggestions as to how he was going to fix the economy. McCain came out rather erratic when he was pushed for an answer which was contrasted by Obama's calm demeanor and preparedness.

On November 4, 2008, there was a massive turnout of voters across the country, and Barack Obama was elected by a comfortable margin to be the President of the United States. He got 53% of the votes to McCain's 46%, and in the Electoral College, he prevailed by a margin of 365. Many first-time voters supported Obama, which helped expand the electorate, and there was massive African American support as expected, electing the first African American chief executive of the country. He carried all the traditionally blue states and flipped several traditionally red states such as Indiana, North Carolina, Virginia, Ohio, and Colorado.

"If there is anyone out there who still doubts that America is a place where all things are possible; who still wonders if the dream of our founders is alive in our time; who still questions the power of our democracy, tonight is your answer." - Election Night Victory Speech, Grant Park, Illinois, November 4, 2008

2012 Presidential Campaign

President Obama and Vice President Joe Biden declared their re-election on April 4, 2011. The digital presence of the Obama administration was quite high, leveraging the booming landscape of social media. Their re-election announcement was made online in a video called "It begins with us." Like many incumbent presidents, President Obama did not face a big challenge in his own party's primaries and easily won the required number of delegates. The campaign slogan was announced to be "Forward." They based the campaign in

Chicago as opposed to Washington DC, where most of the modern presidents based their re-election campaigns. This was done as a way to ensure there would be grassroots support for the campaign, which was one of the biggest reasons he won his previous presidential election.

When President Obama was entering the election year 2012, his job approval ratings were some of the lowest during his entire tenure. The unemployment rate of the country was also quite high. However, just like many other previous incumbent presidents who were running for re-election and won, he benefited from not having to battle for his own party's nomination in the primaries. He used the first eight months of the re-election campaign to fundraise and rebuild his campaign organization, starting the first campaign fundraiser in Chicago. It is claimed that the 2012 Obama presidential campaign was the first campaign in the history of the US to raise over one billion dollars. A notable fundraiser was the one the popular actor George Clooney hosted in his Los Angeles home, which reportedly raised about $15 million for the campaign. It was around the same time the Obama administration made a historic announcement of his support for same-sex marriage, which largely contributed to the fundraising number since the LGBTQ community and activists made historical donations.

Keeping up with the expanding tech and social media need for almost every aspect of political campaigning, Obama's 2012 campaign put together a skilled team of developers from almost all the major tech companies in the US, including Google, Facebook, and Twitter. Harper Reed was the CTO for the campaign, and he took up a whole new approach in putting together his campaign team, which was different from any of the previous presidential campaigns. The central component of Reed's tech work for the campaign was creating a centralized database of all the electoral information. Reed was joined by Dan Wagner, an expert analyst who worked as the Chief Analytics Officer. He had a large analytics team of over fifty people, and they worked in a closed room called the "cave," in which they made remarkably accurate result predictions.

The battle within the Republican Party to choose their nominee helped the Obama campaign quite a lot. While Massachusetts governor Mitt Romney won the nomination, his opponents in the primary battle included the former Speaker Newt Gingrich. Gingrich accused Romney of defrauding companies during his career as a business consultant. Another opponent of his attacked Romney's wealth, accusing him of getting rich by being fraudulent against others. Even once Romney got the nomination, his opponents did not back him the way Obama's opponents did during his 2008 campaign, which contributed to consistent bad poll numbers on Romney's part. However, with strong Republican and Democratic strongholds in the country, Obama and Romney expected to win about twenty states each without much competition. They fought on ten battleground states that were expected to go either way. The battleground states included large states such as Florida and Ohio, and smaller states such as Iowa and New Hampshire. Just like it was predicted in the previous campaign, a win in Iowa was crucial to have a clear path to victory, even if it was a small state.

Just like in the 2008 election, the Get Out the Vote (GOTV) efforts by the Obama 2012 campaign were quite effective. They used more and more technology to identify the voters and capitalize successfully on growing segments of the American voting population. The campaign targeted segments separately based on geographical locations, age, race, gender, and more. Obama participated in four debates held in locations across

America. There was a large political impact of Hurricane Sandy that directly affected the presidential campaign as well. President Obama received nationwide praise for the way he reacted to the tragedy.

On November 6, 2012, Barack Obama was re-elected for his second term as the POTUS. He won 332 electoral votes, which meant he lost two states that he won in his 2008 victory. In his victory speech, he emphasized that he would work towards a bipartisan future for the United States of America.

Chapter 7: What Might be Next for Obama

"The best way to not feel hopeless is to get up and do something. Don't wait for a good thing to happen to you." - Barack Obama.

At noon on January 20, 2017, Barack Obama's presidency ended when Donald Trump was inaugurated to be the President of the United States. Both Obama and Biden attended Trump's inauguration and also graciously extended the courtesy of inviting the President-Elect to the White House prior to the inauguration to welcome him and the family as the new occupants of the people's house. Once the inauguration was over, President Obama was lifted off on the Marine One helicopter, which circled the White House and flew to Joint Base Andrews. He and the family had decided to stay in Washington DC until their youngest daughter graduated from high school.

Travels

Right after Obamas left the white house, the first order of business was to take a much-needed vacation. Even in the farewell interviews President Obama had as his second term in office came to an end, he kept speaking enthusiastically about the travel plans he had, expressing his desire to take his wife on a long vacation. The first publicized travel adventure after the White House was a star-studded trip the Obamas had with a few of their close friends, including big names such as Tom

Hanks, Oprah, and Bruce Springsteen. The travels included exotic and sunny parts of the world, such as Tahiti and French Polynesia. They apparently vacationed in a luxury resort in a private French Polynesian island, which used to be owned by Marlon Brando.

As the US was being introduced to the Trump administration, President Obama spent time traveling in Europe. His tours were both for work and for pleasure. He stopped in a few European golf courses, including the prestigious Old Course at St. Andrew's in Scotland. He also met with German Chancellor Angela Merkel at the Brandenburg Gate in Berlin, with who he had formed a close friendship during his presidency. He also had a long and happy vacation in Italy with Michelle and caused a happy stir in social media when the images of their vacation were published. During his travels in Europe, he also stopped by the Kensington Palace in Britain, where he had a meeting with Prince Harry, among others.

Perhaps one of the most special traveling experiences after he left office, President Obama took his wife and daughters on a trip to Bali, Indonesia. The beautiful South East Asian Island had a special place in Obama's life since he had spent a considerable portion of his childhood in Indonesia with his then stepfather. Later the same year, Obama attended the Invictus Games, where Prince Harry and the Bidens joined him. He also gave an interview with Prince Harry, speaking about his life after the White House and social issues such as healthcare and education in the US that he still cares about.

Presidential Center

The Barack Obama Presidential Center is the planned presidential library of Barack Obama, situated in Jackson Park, Chicago. The location chosen was close to the University of Chicago campus and on the South Side of Chicago, close to the heart of the Obama family. Within the center, there is a plan to have a new branch of the Chicago Public Library as well. The presidential center building is overseen by the Obama Foundation, a non-profit organization that focuses on charity work and other programs by Barack and Michelle Obama. The Presidential Center also plans to partner up with the National Archives and Records Administration to digitize the records taken during the eight years Obama held office. The construction of the presidential library began in early 2021.

The side selection for the presidential library was carefully made, with several bids coming from locations important in Barack Obama's life, including the University of Hawaii, President Obama's home state, and Columbia University, New York, where he completed his bachelor's degree. The board of the presidential library selected the University of Chicago because President Obama had many memories in the university when he was working as a constitutional law professor from 1992 to 2004. Once the partnership with the University of Chicago was established, the board looked for exact locations in which it would be built. The possible locations were Washington Park or Jackson Park. The latter was eventually selected.

A team of renowned architects was selected to plan and design the presidential library, including sculptor Don Gummer, the spouse of the popular actress Meryl Streep. Other personnel in the design advisory committee included Ed Schlossberg, Fred

Eychaner, and Margaret Russell, the Architectural Digest Magazine editor. The local community reaction to the presidential center was quite positive. The building and maintenance of the library and the attraction it will make for tourists will bring more jobs to the neighborhood, support and create businesses, and strengthen the neighborhood schools.

The Obama Foundation

The Barack Obama Foundation is a non-profit organization based in Chicago. Apart from overseeing the building of the presidential center of Barack Obama, it runs several charity programs and offers scholarships for promising students. According to Obama, the purpose of the foundation is to be central to many of his social work and other activities after his presidency. The foundation had raised over $200 million in 2017, according to its filed annual report. The first president of the foundation was a Nigerian economist called Adewale Adeyemo, who was later replaced by Valerie Jarrett, a long-term friend of Obama.

My Brother's Keeper Alliance is another major project handled by the Obama Foundation. It started during his presidency, and he decided to carry it and fund it through his foundation after seeing the positive impact it made on young men of color. It started off as a public and private partnership, promoting intervention by civic leaders in the lives of young men. The initiative involved mayors, tribal leaders, and county executives to recognize and fill the opportunity gaps for young men of color, helping them reach their full potential. The Obama Foundation works towards providing education and mentoring and job training, and many other activities that help young people make a successful move from education to the job market.

The Obama Foundation announced a scholarship program in 2018 in partnership with the University of Chicago. The scholarship is aimed at twenty-five master's students in the Harris School of Public Policy under the University of Chicago. Scholarships can be obtained by both American and International students who are focused on issues of global importance in their graduate research. The students are also required to have a proven track record and commitment to advancing the public good in order to accelerate their impact. The scholarship includes full tuition along with a stipend for living expenses.

Politics

Apart from the many post-presidential social work and other projects lined up for him, Barack Obama has remained involved in politics. He mostly provides endorsements and releases statements on social and political issues that are important to him. He was awarded the Profile in Courage Award given by the John F. Kennedy Presidential Library and Museum in 2017. He has made public appearances in seminars, with his first appearance being at the University of Chicago. During the 2017 French Presidential Election, he publicly endorsed Emmanuel Macron, a centrist politician, over the right-wing populist opposing him. Shortly after, he made a joint public appearance with German Chancellor Angela Merkel in her re-election campaign. He also met with Prince Harry in Kensington Palace in England to discuss their foundations.

He made a major statement against the Trump administration's decision to withdraw from the Paris agreement. When the Senate Republicans put forth a draft to replace the Affordable Care Act, Obama released a statement saying how the new bill would be a transfer of wealth from the middle-class and poor families to the richest people in America. Another legislation issue he spoke out about was against the DACA program's termination that he introduced during his tenure. He went on an international trip that covered China, India, and France, delivering speeches at the Global Alliance of SMEs Summit and the Hindustan Times Leadership Summit. He also attended a town hall for young leaders organized by his foundation. When President Trump made a decision to withdraw from the nuclear deal with Iran in 2018, he criticized it, saying that the deal was in US interests and that withdrawing from it would only bring harm. Moving on to the 2020 election year, he made many appearances in support of his former VP Joe Biden's presidential bid.

The 2020 Election

As a close friend and ally of the democratic presidential nominee Joe Biden, former President Barack Obama was a central figure in the 2020 presidential race. As a widely respected former president, he was eagerly embraced by the Democratic Party and supporters, especially since he is closely connected with Joe Biden after spending eight years by his side. Young and minority supporters were a strong force when electing President Obama, and his involvement in the Biden campaign helped bring that demographic out to support Biden as well. The Biden presidential campaign made Obama a highly visible figure, especially during the last few months running up to the election.

The public and visible involvement of Barack and Michelle Obama in the Biden campaign led to then-President Trump making personal attacks. However, the Biden campaign used those attacks and stated how President Trump was erratic towards Obama only as a desperate measure to distract the public from his own failures. Even though he had avoided making overt comments on President Trump during the first two or three years, he made clear and direct comments that became quite useful for the Biden campaign during his campaign appearances. He was not yet another surrogate who supported Joe Biden, but was a unique ambassador who was a respected and believable voice that the country had grown to trust.

President Trump continued accusing Obama of being guilty of crimes without ever specifying which crimes he was talking about. Apart from attacking the policy issues of the Trump administration, Obama was quite particularly critical about the way they handled the coronavirus pandemic.

A Promised Land

A Promised Land is the much-coveted memoir by Barack Obama, which was published a few months after the highly successful memoir *Becoming* by his wife, Michelle Obama. It was the first of a planned two-volume series. The book speaks the story of his life from his childhood to the events surrounding Osama Bin Laden's killing. This was his third memoir. He had published his first memoir, *Dreams from My Father*, after he was made the first African American editor of the Harvard Law Review. His second book, *The Audacity of Hope*, was published two years before his presidential run. This book follows the tradition of releasing a memoir within a few years of leaving the White House, which started after Calvin Coolidge left the office in 1929.

The content of the book is "an honest accounting of my presidency," as stated by President Obama. He speaks about the forces America grapples with as a nation and how to heal the superficial divisions and make democracy work for everyone. He starts the book by speaking about his early life, with a little detail into the years as a lawyer and when he met Michelle. Then, he gives a detailed look at his campaigns and his experiences as the President until well into his first term. Some of the highlights include his college years when he used to read works of philosophers to his potential love interests. He then gives honest descriptions of other politicians such as Joe Biden and Hillary Clinton and the friendships he made.

Academics and the public alike favorably received the book. Many writers who had read the book praised Obama for his writing skills, and he was quite adamant on mentioning that he was the writer of the book and did not use a ghostwriter like many politicians, including Donald Trump, did when they published books.

Netflix and Spotify

In 2018, Barack and Michelle Obama signed a deal with Netflix to produce TV series and movies, with the potential to work on both scripted and unscripted documentary films and features. The multi-year deal will include productions from their company, Higher Ground Productions. They released a joint statement saying that they love meeting people from different walks of life and that they hope to help them share their experiences through the productions they will be doing to share those experiences with a wider audience. They further added that they hope to cultivate and curate the talented and inspiring creative voices who are able to promote greater understanding between people, helping them share their stories with the world.

They signed another deal with Spotify to produce a series of podcasts exclusively for the platform. The deal included the idea that stories should be produced to give people that are missed or underrepresented a voice. In a statement, he added that he had always believed in the value of entertaining and thought-provoking conversation. It helps us build connections with each other and open ourselves up to new ideas. He also added that he hopes to bring people together with the help of the podcasts that he plans to produce. One of his first projects on the platform was a podcast called "Renegades: Born in the USA" with Bruce Springsteen. The name of the podcast was a nod to both Obama's secret service name and the popular song by Springsteen.

With Netflix and Spotify, the Obamas have audiences worldwide that surpass hundreds of millions of viewers and listeners.

Conclusion

"It took a lot of blood, sweat, and tears to get to where we are today, but we have just begun. Today we begin in earnest the work of making sure that the world we leave our children is just a little bit better than the one we inhabit today." - Barack Obama

Born to a white mother from Hawaii and a black father from Kenya, Barack Obama spent a confused adolescence trying to figure out his identity in the world. He pulled himself up by his bootstraps by studying and working hard to elevate his social status and has walked a path to the White House that few presidents have walked before. Obama was raised by his mother with the help of her parents, who generously contributed to his education and instilled homespun Midwestern values that he carried with him all along. Obama was aware of the extraordinary chance America gave him, and his work reflected how he wanted to make the same story true for every child who came from similar backgrounds.

He worked his way through college with the help of student loans and scholarships until receiving his Juris Doctor degree from Harvard Law School. His first instinct was to work as a community organizer. The experience he had in working with impoverished communities in Chicago honed his belief in the inherent power of uniting ordinary people around a purpose that feels closer to them. He learned the importance of hard work in order to bring about positive and lasting change.

As an African American man who reached the country's highest office, Barack Obama has been many "firsts." He became the first African American President of the Harvard Law Review at the age of twenty-eight. It took the prestigious school 104 years to finally take that historic step. Once he graduated from Harvard with a JD degree magna cum laude, he returned to Chicago to teach constitutional law at the University of Chicago. It did not take him long to start a career in public service when he ran for the state senate seat in Illinois and won. He then ran for United States Senate representing Illinois, which he won. On November 4, 2008, Barack Obama defeated Arizona Senator John McCain and won with more votes than any candidate in history at that time.

America was going through a distressing moment of crisis when Barack Hussein Obama pledged to faithfully execute the office of President of the United States on a clear January morning in 2009. With Michelle Obama by his side, he pledged to preserve, protect, and defend the United States Constitution to the best of his ability. The nation was at war at the time, and the planet was in peril, with vital signs of climate change appearing across the world. With the Great Recession's burden upon the country, the American Dream itself was highly threatened. Even with plenty of political obstruction during the eight years he was in office, he led the country away from the economic collapse and revitalized the job market and the auto industry that had been hit hard during the previous administration's recession. Reforming healthcare was yet another achievement, which remained to be one of his first priorities since he took office. The Affordable Care Act, or "Obamacare," was able to help give affordable health care coverage to tens of millions of Americans, and it continues to expand coverage and ensure that people with pre-existing conditions can get insured.

President Obama carried out a strong and principled diplomacy in resolving many global issues that occurred on the world stage. He helped wind down not one but two wars—in Iraq and

Afghanistan—and as the commander-in-chief, he oversaw Osama bin Laden's killing, one of the world's most wanted terrorists. He also made a historical deal that blocked Iran from acquiring nuclear weapons. Taking leadership in the world's coordinated action towards combating climate change is another noteworthy achievement during the Obama presidency. Prof. Katherine A. Sibley, a History professor at St. Joseph's University, likens Obama to former US presidents John F. Kennedy and Dwight Eisenhower. She says he brought relative youth, hope, and inspiration to the White House while being strategic and pragmatic in his actions at the same time.

When Barack Obama addressed the crowd gathered at Chicago's Grant Park back in 2008, delivering his victory speech and saying, "Change has come to America," it was a moment etched into the history of the United States of America forever. He might have been a conventional president with a mixed assessment by political pundits and historians alike, but it is undeniable that he had an extraordinary capacity to tap into the deepest hopes and aspirations of the American people, creating a broad and varied coalition that rivaled many US presidents before him. Barack Obama's ascent to the highest office of the land was absolutely inspiring. He was almost like a rock star to a progressive generation that had an innately liberal view of the world, even though their parents were largely conservative. Obama's image as a political leader striving for real change in the world was the image the Millennials had when it came to their political representatives.

With laser-like focus, he tried to change the way the American people thought about the government. While he may not have succeeded entirely, and there will always be more work to do to achieve a better America, Barack Hussein Obama will always be remembered as a president with integrity, dignity, and grace.

Lightning Source UK Ltd.
Milton Keynes UK
UKHW020710210622
404740UK00011B/1071